JOHN
to
ABIGAIL

JOHN
to
ABIGAIL

Selected Letters of John Adams

Book-of-the-Month Club
New York

The letters here have been taken from *Letters of John Adams,*
Addressed to his Wife, Volumes I and II, edited by Charles
Francis Adams.

Ellipses are used to indicate where a portion of a letter has
been excerpted.

Edited by Ben Hallman

This edition was especially created in 2001 for Book-of-the-
Month Club. This edition copyright © 2001 by Bookspan.
All rights reserved.

Book design by Ben Hallman

Printed in U.S.A.

CONTENTS

INTRODUCTION

John Adams is one of the great witnesses to the life of his times as well as one of its key participants. He loved great literature and was an ardent reader, and in a tranquil era he might have become a contented country lawyer and farmer who composed verse in his spare time. Instead, drawn away from the homestead and frequently separated from his "best friend," his wife Abigail, he addressed her as often as possible in a series of wonderful letters.

It is in these letters that we learn Adams's opinions of the Continental Congress, his impressions of Europe where he represented the fledgling nation, and his view of the tumultuous politics of the new republic when he served as George Washington's vice president. Fearful of interceptions and espionage—and rightly so—he sometimes restrained his legendary candor in these letters, but even at his most circumspect, Adams is a compelling correspondent. His forceful spirit always comes through, so different from the reserve of Washington or the veil of style behind which Jefferson hid. It is in these letters that we also discern the loving husband and father. To read Adams's letters is to become acquainted with the man.

Our selection ends with Adams's retirement from politics and return to the farm at Quincy, Massachusetts. Still to come were the great outpouring of letters he wrote to Jefferson when they resumed their strained friendship. That is perhaps a collection for another occasion.

I

FIRST CONTINENTAL CONGRESS

After England passed the Intolerable Acts in 1774, the Sons of Liberty and the committees of correspondence resolved to form an intercolonial assembly to address the problem, much like the one assembled nine years earlier following the imposition of the hated Stamp Act.

Delegates from all colonies but Georgia were represented when the First Continental Congress, as it came to be known, met in Carpenters Hall in Philadelphia on September 5, 1774. Although the only major act of the new Congress was the formation of the Continental Association, which promptly declared illegal the importation of all British goods and restricted the export of certain colonial exports, it served as an important introduction to the colonial leaders of the upcoming revolution.

Philadelphia, 14 September 1774

My Dear,

I have written but once to you since I left you. This is to be imputed to a variety of causes, which I cannot explain for want of time. It would fill volumes to give you an exact idea of the whole tour. My time is totally filled from the moment I get out of bed until I return to it. Visits, ceremonies, company, business, newspapers, pamphlets, &c., &c., &c.

The Congress will, to all present appearance, be well united, and in such measures as, I hope, will give satisfaction to the friends of our country. A Tory here is the most despicable animal in the creation. Spiders, toads, snakes are their only proper emblems. The Massachusetts Councillors and Addressers are held in curious esteem here, as you will see. The spirit, the firmness, the prudence of our province are vastly applauded, and we are universally acknowledged, the saviours and defenders of American liberty. The designs and plans of the Congress must not be communicated until completed, and we shall move with great deliberation.

When I shall come home I know not, but at present, I do not expect to take my leave of this city these four weeks. My compliments, love, service, where they are due. My babes are never out of my mind, nor absent from my heart.

Adieu.
John Adams

Philadelphia, 20 September 1774

My Dear,

I am very well yet. Write to me as often as you can, and send your letters to the office in Boston, or to Mr. Cranch's [Richard, Adams's brother-in-law], where they will be sent by the first conveyance.

I am anxious to know how you can live without government. But the experiment must be tried. The evils will not be found so dreadful as you apprehend them. Frugality, my dear, frugality, economy, parsimony, must be our refuge. I hope the ladies are every day diminishing their ornaments, and the gentlemen too. Let us eat potatoes, and drink water. Let us wear canvass, and undressed sheepskins, rather than submit to the unrighteous, and ignominious domination that is prepared for us.

Tell Brackett I shall make him leave off drinking rum. We can't let him fight yet. My love to my dear ones.

Adieu.
John Adams

Philadelphia, 25 September 1774

My Dear,

I would not lose the opportunity of writing to you, though I must be short.

Tedious indeed is our business—slow as snails. I have not been used to such ways. We sit only before dinner. We dine at four o'clock. We are crowded with a levee in the evening.

Fifty gentlemen meeting together, all strangers, are not acquainted with each other's language, ideas, views, designs. They are therefore jealous of each other—fearful, timid, skittish.

Philadelphia, 9 October 1774

My Dear,

I am wearied to death with the life I lead. The business of the Congress is tedious beyond expression. This assembly is like no other that ever existed. Every man in it is a great man, an orator, a critic, a statesman; and therefore, every man upon every question, must show his oratory, his criticism, and his political abilities. The consequence of this is, that business is drawn and spun out to an immeasurable length. I believe, if it was moved and seconded, that we should come to a resolution that three and two make five, we should be entertained with logic, and rhetoric, law, history, politics and mathematics, and then—we should pass the resolution, unanimously, in the affirmative. The perpetual round of feasting too, which we are obliged to submit to, makes the pilgrimage more tedious to me.

This day, I went to Dr. Allison's meeting in the forenoon, and heard the Dr.; a good discourse upon the Lord's supper. This is a Presbyterian meeting. I confess I am not fond of the Presbyterian meetings in this town. I had rather go to church. We have better sermons, better prayers, better speakers, softer, sweeter music, and genteeler company. And I must confess, that the Episcopal church is quite as agreeable to my taste as the Presbyterian. They are both slaves to the domination of the priesthood. I like the Congregational way best; next to that, the Independent.

This afternoon, led by a curiosity and good company, I strolled away to mother church, or rather, grandmother church. I mean the Romish Chapel. I heard a good, short, moral essay upon the duty of parents to their children founded in justice and charity, to take care of their interests, temporal and spiritual. This afternoon's entertainment was to me most awful and affecting. The poor wretches fingering their beads, chanting Latin, not a word of which they understood; their pater nosters and ave Marias; their holy water; their crossing themselves perpetually; their bowing to the name of Jesus, wherever they hear it; their bowings, and kneelings, and genuflections before the altar. The dress of the priest was rich with lace. His pulpit was velvet and gold. The altar-piece was very rich; little images and crucifixes about; wax candles lighted up. But how shall I describe the picture of our Saviour, in a frame of marble over the altar, at full length, upon the cross in the agonies, and the blood dropping and streaming from his wounds! The music, consisting of an organ and a choir of singers, went all the afternoon, except sermon time. And the assembly chanted most sweetly and exquisitely.

Here is everything which can lay hold of the eye, ear, and imagination. Everything which can charm, and bewitch the simple and ignorant. I wonder how Luther ever broke the spell.

Adieu.
John Adams

II

Second Continental Congress

The Second Continental Congress met on May 10, 1775—this time with all colonies represented—in the immediate aftermath of the battles of Lexington and Concord. The mood was somber, yet the majority of the delegates still favored reconciliation with England.

John Adams emerged as an energized and capable leader of the "radicals"—the vocal minority. He had only recently come to the conclusion that independence was the key to the restoration of liberties in America, but he was outstandingly effective in his efforts to sway others to his side. It was Adams who championed George Washington to command the new Continental Army, which was at least partially a bid to bind Virginia more tightly to the cause of independence. He worked day and night, not only to drum up support for a formal break with England, but also to create a working and unified government out of thirteen bickering, divided Colonies.

Philadelphia, 17 June 1775

. . . I can now inform you, that the Congress have made choice of the modest and virtuous, the amiable, generous and brave George Washington, Esquire, to be General of the American army, and that he is to repair, as soon as possible, to the camp before Boston. This appointment will have a great effect in cementing and securing the union of these colonies. The continent is really in earnest, in defending the country. They have voted ten companies of riflemen to be sent from Pennsylvania, Maryland and Virginia, to join the army before Boston. These are an excellent species of light infantry. They use a peculiar kind of musket, called a rifle. It has circular or [word missing] grooves within the barrel, and carries a ball with great exactness to great distances. They are the most accurate marksmen in the world.

I begin to hope we shall not sit all summer. I hope the people of our province will treat the General with all that confidence and affection, that politeness and respect, which is due to one of the most important characters in the world. The liberties of America depend upon him, in a great degree. I have never been able to obtain from our province any regular and particular intelligence since I left it. Kent, Swift, Tudor, Dr. Cooper, Dr. Winthrop [friends in Massachusetts with whom Adams frequently corresponded] and others wrote me often last fall; not a line from them this time.

I have found this Congress like the last. When we first came together, I found a strong jealousy of us from New England, and the Massachusetts in particular. Suspicions entertained of designs of independency; an American republic; presbyterian principles, and twenty other things. Our sentiments were heard in Congress with great caution, and seemed to make but little impression; but the longer we sat, the more clearly they saw the necessity of pushing vigorous measures. It has been so now. Every day we sit, the more we are convinced that the designs against us are hostile and sanguinary, and that nothing but fortitude, vigor, and perseverance can save us. . . .

Philadelphia, 23 July 1775

My Dear,

You have more than once, in your letters, mentioned Dr.
Franklin, and in one, intimated a desire that I should write
you something concerning him.

Dr. Franklin has been very constant in his attendance
on Congress from the beginning. His conduct has been
composed and grave, and, in the opinion of many gentlemen, very reserved. He has not assumed any thing, nor
affected to take the lead; but has seemed to choose that the
Congress should pursue their own principles and sentiments, and adopt their own plans. Yet he has not been
backward; has been very useful on many occasions, and
discovered a disposition entirely American. He does not
hesitate at our boldest measures, but rather seems to think
us too irresolute and backward. He thinks us at present in
an odd state, neither in peace nor war, neither dependent
nor independent; but he thinks that we shall soon assume a
character more decisive. He thinks that we have the power
of preserving ourselves; and that even if we should be dri-
ven to the disagreeable necessity of assuming a total independency, and set up a separate state, we can maintain it.
The people of England have thought that the opposition in
America, was wholly owing to Dr. Franklin; and I suppose
their scribblers will attribute the temper and proceedings of
Congress to him; but there cannot be a greater mistake. He
has had but little share, further than to cooperate and to
assist. He is however a great and good man. I wish his colleagues from this city were all like him; particularly one,[1]
whose abilities and virtues, formerly trumpeted so much in

---

[1] An allusion to John Dickinson. He had labored hard and successfully to procure the adoption, by Congress, of a second petition to the King, against the
opinion of many among the more zealous patriots. This gave rise to the idea
that he was lukewarm to the cause of resistance.

America, have been found wanting. There is a young gentleman from Pennsylvania, whose name is [James] Wilson, whose fortitude, rectitude and abilities too, greatly outshine his master's. Mr. [Clement] Biddle, the Speaker, has been taken off by sickness, Mr. [Thomas] Mifflin is gone to the camp, Mr. [John] Morton is ill too, so that this province has suffered by the timidity of two overgrown fortunes. The dread of confiscation or caprice, I know not what, has influenced them to much; yet they were for taking arms, and pretended to be very valiant.

This letter must be secret, my dear; at least, communicated with great discretion.

Yours,
John Adams

[Philadelphia] 29 October 1775

Human nature with all its infirmities and depravation is still capable of great things. It is capable of attaining to degrees of wisdom and of goodness, which, we have reason to believe, appear respectable in the estimation of superior intelligences. Education makes a greater difference between man and man, than nature has made between man and brute. The virtues and powers to which men may be trained, by early education and constant discipline, are truly sublime and astonishing. Newton and Locke are examples of the deep sagacity which may be acquired by long habits of thinking and study. Nay, your common mechanics and artisans are proofs of the wonderful dexterity acquired by use; a watchmaker, in finishing his wheels and springs, a pin or needlemaker, &c. I think there is a particular occupation in Europe, which is called a paper-stainer or linen-stainer. A man who has been long habituated to it, shall sit for a whole day, and draw upon paper fresh figures to be imprinted upon the papers for rooms, as fast as his eye can roll, and his fingers move, and no two of his draughts shall be alike. The Saracens, the Knights of Malta, the army and navy in the service of the English republic, among many others, are instances to show, to what an exalted height valor or bravery or courage may be raised, by artificial means.

It should be your care, therefore, and mine, to elevate the minds of our children and exalt their courage; to accelerate and animate their industry and activity; to excite in them an habitual contempt of meanness, abhorrence of injustice and inhumanity, and an ambition to excel in every capacity, faculty and virtue. If we suffer their minds to grovel and creep in infancy, they will grovel all their lives.

But their bodies must be hardened, as well as their souls exalted. Without strength and activity and vigor of body, the brightest mental excellencies will be eclipsed and obscured.

[Philadelphia] 3 December 1775

My Best Friend,

Yours of November 12th is before me. I wish I could write you every day, more than once, for although I have a number of friends and many relations, who are very dear to me, yet all the friendship I have for others is far unequal to that which warms my heart for you. The most agreeable time that I spend here is in writing to you, and conversing with you, when I am alone. But the call of friendship and of private affection must give place to that of duty and honor. Even private friendship and affections require it.

I am obliged, by the nature of the service I am in, to correspond with many gentlemen, both of the army and of the two houses of Assembly, which takes up much of my time. How I find time to write half the letters I do, I know not, for my whole time seems engrossed with business. The whole Congress is taken up, almost, in different committees, from seven to ten in the morning. From ten to four or sometimes five, we are in Congress, and from six to ten, in committees again. I don't mention this to make you think me a man of importance, because it is not I alone, but the whole Congress is thus employed, but to apologize for not writing to you oftener. . . .

As to coming home I have no thoughts of it; shall stay here till the year is out, for what I know. Affairs are in a critical state, and important steps are now taking every day, so that I could not reconcile it to my own mind to be absent from this place at present. Nothing is expected from the Commissioners, yet we are waiting for them in some respects. The tories and timids pretend to expect great things from them. But the generality expect nothing but more insults and affronts. Privateering is licensed, and the ports are wide open. As soon as the resolves are printed, which will be tomorrow, I will send them.

Philadelphia, 18 February 1776

My Dearest Friend,

I sent you from New York a pamphlet intituled "Common Sense,"[2] written in vindication of doctrines, which there is reason to expect, that the further encroachments of tyranny and depredations of oppression will soon make the common faith; unless the cunning ministry, by proposing negotiations and terms of reconciliation, should divert the present current from its channel.

Reconciliation if practicable, and peace if attainable, you very well know, would be as agreeable to my inclina-

---

[2] Tremendously successful pro-revolution pamphlet written by Thomas Paine. Argued that the colonies had outgrown their need for English rule, and should be independent. Adams was flattered to learn that many in Massachusetts believed him to be the author.

tions, and as advantageous to my interest, as to any man's. But I see no prospect, no probability, no possibility. And I cannot but despise the understanding, which sincerely expects an honorable peace, for its credulity, and detest the hypocritical heart, which pretends to expect it, when in truth it does not. The newspapers here are full of free speculations, the tendency of which you will easily discover. The writers reason from topics which have been long in contemplation and fully understood by the people at large in New England, but have been attended to in the southern colonies only by gentlemen of free spirits and liberal minds, who are very few. I shall endeavour to enclose to you as many of the papers and pamphlets as I can, as long as I stay here. Some will go by the conveyance.

Dr. Franklin, Mr. Chase,[3] and Mr. Charles Carroll of Carrollton in Maryland, are chosen a committee to go into Canada. The characters of the two first you know. The last is not a member of Congress, but a gentleman of independent fortune, perhaps the largest in America, a hundred and fifty or two hundred thousand pounds sterling; educated in some university in France, though a native of America, of great abilities and learning, complete master of the French language, and a professor of the Roman Catholic religion, yet a warm, a firm, a zealous supporter of the rights of America, in whose cause he has hazarded his all. Mr. John Carroll, of Maryland, a Roman Catholic priest and a Jesuit, is to go with the committee; the priests in Canada having refused baptism and absolution to our friends there. General Lee is to command in that country, whose address, experience and abilities, added to his fluency in the French language, will give him great advantages.

The events of war are uncertain. We cannot ensure success, but we can deserve it. I am happy in this provision for that important department, because I think it the best that

---

[3] Samuel Chase, revolutionary political leader and future Supreme Court Justice.

could be made in our circumstances. Your prudence will direct you to communicate the circumstances of the priest, the jesuit, and the Romish religion, only to such persons as can judge of the measure upon large and generous principles, and will not indiscreetly divulge it. The step was necessary, for the anathemas of the church are very terrible to our friends in Canada.

I wish I understood French as well as you. I would have gone to Canada, if I had. I feel the want of education every day, particularly of that language. I pray, my dear, that you would not suffer your sons or your daughter ever to feel a similar pain. It is in your power to teach them French, and I, every day, see more and more, that it will become a necessary accomplishment of an American gentleman or lady. Pray write me in your next the name of the author of your thin French grammar, which gives you the pronunciation of the French words in English letters, that is, which shows you how the same sounds would be signified by English vowels and consonants.

Write me as often as you can. Tell me all the news. Desire the children to write to me, and believe me to be theirs and yours.

[Philadelphia] 19 March 1776

Yesterday I had the long expected and much wished pleasure of a letter from you, of various dates from the 2d to the 10th March. This is the first line I have received since I left you. I wrote you from Watertown, I believe, relating my feast at the Quarter Master General's with the Caghnawaga Indians,[4] and from New York I sent you a pamphlet. Hope you received these. Since I arrived here, I have written to you as often as I could.

---

[4] Iroquois Indians from Caghnawaga, a hamlet in the Hudson Valley.

I am much pleased with your caution in your letter, in avoiding names both of persons and places, or any other circumstances, which might designate to strangers the writer, or the person written to, or the persons mentioned. Characters and description will do as well.

The lie which, you say, occasioned such disputes at the tavern, was curious enough. Who could make and spread it? I am much obliged to an uncle for his friendship. My worthy fellow citizens may be easy about me. I never can forsake what I take to be their interests. My own have never been considered by me in competition with theirs. My ease, my domestic happiness, my rural pleasures, my little property, my personal liberty, my reputation, my life have little weight and ever had in my own estimation, in comparison of the great object of my country. I can say of it with sincerity, as Horace says of virtue. "To America only and her friends a friend."

You ask what is thought of "Common Sense." Sensible men think there are some whims, some sophisms, some artful addresses to superstitious notions, some keen attempts upon the passions, in this pamphlet. But all agree there is a great deal of good sense delivered in clear, simple, concise and nervous style. His sentiments of the abilities of America, and of the difficulty of a reconciliation with Great Britain, are generally approved. But his notions and plans of continental government are not much applauded. Indeed this writer has a better hand in pulling down than building. It has been very generally propagated through the continent that I wrote this pamphlet. But although I could not have written anything in so manly and striking a style, I flatter myself I should have made a more respectable figure as an architect, if I had undertaken such a work. This writer seems to have very inadequate ideas of what is proper and necessary to be done, in order to form constitutions for single colonies, as well as a great model of union for the whole. . . .

Philadelphia, 15 April 1776

I send you every newspaper that comes out, and I send you, now and then, a few sheets of paper, but this article is as scarce here, as with you. I would send a quire, if I could get a conveyance.

I write you now and then a line, as often as I can, but I can tell you no news, but what I send in the public papers.

We are waiting, it is said, for commissioners; a messiah that will never come. This story of commissioners is as arrant an illusion as ever was hatched in the brain of an enthusiast, a politician, or a maniac. I have laughed at it, scolded at it, grieved at it, and I don't know but I may, at an unguarded moment, have rip'd at it. But it is vain to reason against such delusions. I was very sorry to see, in a letter from the General, that he had been bubbled with it; and still more to see, in a letter from my sagacious friend, W. [James Warren] at Plymouth, that he was taken in too.

My opinion is, that the commissioners and the commission have been here (I mean in America), these two months. The Governors, Mandamus Councillors, Collectors and Comptrollers and Commanders of the army and navy, I conjecture, compose the list, and their power is to receive submissions. But we are not in a very submissive mood. They will get no advantage of us. We shall go on to perfection, I believe. I have been very busy for some time; have written about ten sheets of paper, with my own hand, about some trifling affairs,[5] which I may mention some time or other—not now, for fear of accidents.

What will come of this labor, time will discover. I shall get nothing by it, I believe, because I never get anything by anything that I do. I am sure the public or posterity ought

---

[5] This probably alludes to "Thoughts on Government," in the form of a letter to George Wythe, of Virginia—a paper that presents a sketch of the governmental system, many elements of which were later incorporated into the Constitution.

to get something. I believe my children will think I might as well have thought and labored a little, night and day, for their benefit. But I will not bear the reproaches of my children. I will tell them, that I studied and labored to procure a free constitution of government for them to solace themselves under, and if they do not prefer this to ample fortune, to ease and elegance, they are not my children, and I care not what becomes of them. They shall live upon thin diet, wear mean clothes, and work hard with cheerful hearts and free spirits, or they may be the children of the earth, or of no one, for me.

John has genius and so has Charles. Take care that they don't go astray. Cultivate their minds, inspire their little hearts, raise their wishes. Fix their attention upon great and glorious objects. Root out every little thing. Weed out every meanness. Make them great and manly. Teach them to scorn injustice, ingratitude, cowardice and falsehood. Let them revere nothing but religion, morality and liberty. . . .

Philadelphia, 3 July 1776

. . . Yesterday, the greatest question was decided, which ever was debated in America, and a greater, perhaps, never was nor will be decided upon men. A Resolution was passed without one dissenting Colony "that these United Colonies are, and of right ought to be, free and independent States, and as such they have, and of right ought to have, full power to make war, conclude peace, establish commerce and to do all other acts and things which other States might rightfully do." You will see, in a few days, a Declaration setting forth the causes which have impelled us to this might revolution, and the reasons which will justify it in the sight of God and man. A plan of confederation will be taken up in a few days.

When I look back to the year 1761 and recollect the argument concerning writs of assistance in the superior court, which I have hitherto considered as the commencement of this controversy between Great Britain and America, and run through the whole period, from that time to this, and recollect the series of political events, the chain of causes and effects, I am surprised at the suddenness, as well as greatness of this revolution. Britain has been filled with folly, and America with wisdom; at least, this is my judgment. Time must determine. It is the will of Heaven that the two countries should be sundered forever. It may be the will of Heaven that America shall suffer calamities still more wasting, and distresses yet more dreadful. If this is to be the case, it will have this good effect at least. It will inspire us with many virtues, which we have not, and correct many errors, follies and vices which threaten to disturb, dishonor, and destroy us. The furnace of affliction produces refinement in states as well as individuals. And the new Governments we are assuming in every part will require a purification from our vices, and an augmentation of our virtues, or they will be no blessings. The people will have unbounded power, and the people are extremely addicted to corruption and venality, as well as the great. But I must submit all my hopes and fears to an overruling providence, in which, unfashionable as the faith may be, I firmly believe.

Philadelphia, 3 July 1776

. . . The second day of July, 1776, will be the most memorable epocha in the history of America. I am apt to believe that it will be celebrated by succeeding generations as the great anniversary Festival [later changed to July 4th, the day on which the form of the declaration was agreed to]. It ought to be commemorated, as the day of deliverance, by solemn acts of devotion to God Almighty. It ought to be solemnized with pomp and parade, with shows, games, sports, guns, bells, bonfires and illuminations, from one end of this continent to the other, from this time forward, forevermore.

You will think me transported with enthusiasm, but I

am not. I am well aware of the toil, and blood, and treasure, that it will cost us to maintain this Declaration, and support and defend these States. Yet, through all the gloom, I can see the rays of ravishing light and glory. I can see that the end is more than worth all the means. And that posterity will triumph in that day's transaction, even although we should rue it, which I trust in God we shall not.

Philadelphia, 27 April 1777

Your favors of April 2d and 7th I have received. The enclosed Evening Post will give you some idea of the humanity of the present race of Britons. My barber, whom I quote as often as ever I did any authority, says, "he has read histories of cruelty and he has read romances of cruelty, but the cruelty of the British exceeds all that he ever read." For my own part I think we cannot dwell too much on this part of their character and conduct. It is full of important lessons. If the facts only were known, in the utmost simplicity of narration, they would strike every pious and humane bosom in Great Britain with horror. Every conscience in that country is not callous, nor every heart hardened. The plainest relation of facts would interest the sympathy and compassion of all Europe in our favor. And it would convince every American, that a nation, so great a part of which is thus deeply depraved, can never be again trusted with power over us. I think that not only history should perform her office, but painting, sculpture, statuary and poetry ought to assist, in publishing to the world and perpetuating to posterity, the horrid deeds of our enemies. It will show the persecution we suffer in defence of our rights; it will show the fortitude, patience, perseverance, and magnanimity of Americans, in as strong a light as the barbarity and impiety of Briton, in this persecuting war. Surely impiety consists in destroying with such hellish barbarity the rational works of the Deity, as much as in blaspheming and defying his majesty.

If there is a moral law, if there is a divine law (and that there is, every intelligent creature is conscious), to trample on these laws, to hold them in contempt and defiance is the highest exertion of wickedness and impiety that mortals can be guilty of. The author of human nature, who can give it its rights, will not see it ruined, and suffer its destroyers to escape with impunity. Divine vengeance will, sometime or other, overtake the Alberts, the Philips and Georges, the Alvas, the Grislers, and Howes, and vindicate the wrongs of oppressed human nature. I think that medals in gold, silver and copper ought to be struck in commemoration of the shocking cruelties, the brutal barbarities, and the diabolical impieties of this war; and these should be contrasted with the kindness, tenderness, humanity and philanthropy which have marked the conduct of Americans towards their prisoners. It is remarkable that the officers and soldiers of our enemies are so totally depraved, so completely destitute of the sentiments of philanthropy in their own hearts, that they cannot believe that such delicate feelings can exist in any other, and therefore have constantly ascribed that milk and honey with which we have treated them, to fear, cowardice and conscious weakness. But in this way they are mistaken, and will discover their mistake too late to answer any good purpose for them.

[Philadelphia], 28 April 1777

There is a clock calm at this time in the political and military hemispheres. The surface is smooth and the air serene. Not a breath nor a wave, no news nor noise.

Nothing would promote our cause more than Howe's march to this town. Nothing quickens and determines people so much as a little smart. The Germans, who are numerous and wealthy in this State, and who have very imperfect ideas of freedom, have a violent attachment to property. They are passionate and vindictive, in a degree that is scarcely credible to persons who are unacquainted with them, and the least injury to their property excites a resentment beyond description. A few houses and plantations plundered (as many would be if Howe should come here), would set them all on fire. Nothing would unite and determine Pennsylvania so effectually. The passions of men must cooperate with their reason in the prosecution of a war. The public may be clearly convinced, that a war is just, and yet, until their passions are excited, will carry it languidly on. The prejudices, the anger, the hatred of the English against the French contributes greatly to their valor and success. The British court and their officers have studied to excite the same passions in the breasts of their soldiers against the Americans, well knowing their powerful effects. We, on the contrary, have treated their characters with too much tenderness. The Howes, their officers, and soldiers too, ought to be held up to the contempt, derision, hatred and abhorrence of the populace in every State, and of the common soldiers in every army. It would give me no pain to see them burned or hanged in effigy, in every town and village.

Philadelphia, 22 May 1777,
4 o'clock in the morning

After a series of the severest and harshest weather that ever I felt in this climate, we are at last blessed with a bright sun and a soft air. The weather here has been like our old easterly winds to me and southerly winds to you. The charms of the morning at this hour are irresistible. The streaks of glory dawning in the east; the freshness and purity in the air, the bright blue of the sky, the sweet warblings of a great variety of birds intermingling with the martial clarions of a hundred cocks now within my hearing, all conspire to cheer the spirits.

This kind of puerile description is a very pretty employment for an old fellow whose brow is furrowed with the cares of politics and war. I shall be on horseback in a few minutes and then I shall enjoy the morning in more perfection. I spent last evening at the war office with General Arnold. He has been basely slandered and libelled. The regulars say, "He fought like Julius Caesar."[6] I am wearied to death with the wrangles between military officers, high and low. They quarrel like cats and dogs. They worry one another like mastiffs, scrambling for rank and pay, like apes for nuts. I believe there is no one principle which predominates in human nature so much, in every stage of life, from the cradle to the grave, in males and females, old and young, black and white, rich and poor, high and low, as this passion for superiority. Every human being compares itself in its imagination with every other round about it, and will find some superiority over every other, real or imaginary, or it will die of grief and vexation. I have seen it among boys and girls at school, among lads at college, among practitioners at the bar, among the clergy in their associations, among clubs of friends, among the people in town meetings, among the members of a House of Representatives, among the grave councillors, on the more solemn bench of Justice, and in that awfully august body, the Congress, and on many of its committees, and among ladies every where; but I never saw it operate with such keenness, ferocity and fury, as among military officers. They will go terrible lengths in their emulation, their envy and revenge, in consequence of it.

So much for philosophy. I hope my five or six babes are all well. My duty to my mother and your father, and love to sisters and brothers, aunts and uncles. Pray how does your asparagus perform? &c. I would give three guineas for a barrel of your cider. Not one drop is to be had here for gold, and wine is not to be had under six or eight dollars a gal-

---

[6] In February of 1777, Congress, despite Washington's protests, promoted five junior officers over Arnold's head. He was eventually made a Major General, but many feel that this, as well as other slights by Congress, led to his later treason.

lon, and that very bad. I would give a guinea for a barrel of your beer. The small beer here is wretchedly bad. In short, I can get nothing that I can drink, and I believe I shall be sick from this cause alone. Rum at forty shillings a gallon, and bad water will never do, in this hot climate, in summer, when acid liquors are necessary against putrefaction.

———

Philadelphia, 25 May 1777

At half past four this morning I mounted my horse and took a ride in a road that was new to me. I went to Kensington and then to "Point-no-point" by land, the place where I went once before with a large company in the row galleys by water. That frolic was almost two years ago. I gave you a relation of it in the time, I suppose. The road to Point-no-point lies along the river Delaware, in fair sight of it and its opposite shore. For near four miles the road is as strait as the streets of Philadelphia. On each side, are beautiful rows of trees, buttonwoods, oaks, walnuts, cherries and willows, especially down towards the banks of the river. The meadows, pastures and grass plats are as green as leeks. There are many fruit trees and fine orchards set with the nicest regularity. But the fields of grain, the rye and wheat exceed all description. These fields are all sown in ridges and the furrow between each couple of ridges is as plainly to be seen as if a swath had been mown along. Yet it is no wider than a ploughshare and it is as strait as an arrow. It looks as if the sower had gone along the furrow with his spectacles to pick up every grain that should accidentally fall into it. The corn is just coming out of the ground. The furrows struck out for the hills to be planted in, are each way as straight, as mathematical right lines; and the squares between every four hills as exact as they could be done by plumb and line, or scale and compass. . . .

Philadelphia, Tuesday 19 August 1777

My Best Friend,

Your obliging favor of the 5th came by yesterday's post, and I intended to have answered it by this morning's post, but was delayed by many matters, until he gave me the slip.

I am sorry that you and the people of Boston were put to so much trouble, but glad to hear that such numbers determined to fly. The prices for carting which were demanded were detestable. I wish your fatigue and anxiety may not have injured your health. Don't be anxious for my safety. If [English General William] Howe comes here, I shall run away, I suppose, with the rest. We are too brittle ware, you know, to stand the dashing of balls and bombs. I wonder upon what principle the Roman senators refused to fly from the Gauls, and determined to sit with their ivory staves and hoary beards, in the porticoes of their houses, until the enemy entered the city and, although they confessed they resembled the gods, put them to the sword. I should not choose to indulge this sort of dignity; but I confess I feel myself so much injured by these barbarian Britons, that I have a strong inclination to meet them in the field. This is not revenge, I believe, but there is something sweet and delicious in the contemplation of it. There is in our hearts an indignation against wrong that is righteous and benevolent; and he who is destitute of it, is defective in the balance of his affections and in his moral character.

As long as there is conscience in our breasts, a moral sense which distinguishes between right and wrong, approving, esteeming, loving the former, and undermining and detesting the other, we must feel a pleasure in the punishment of so eminent a contemner of all that is right, and good, and just, as Howe is. They are virtuous and pious passions that prompt us to desire his destruction, and to lament and deplore his success and prosperity. The desire of assisting towards his disgrace is an honest wish.

It is too late in life, my constitution is too much debilitated by speculation, and indeed, it is too late a period in the war, for me to think of girding on a sword. But if I had the last four years to run over again, I certainly would.

———

York Town, Pennsylvania
Tuesday, 30 September 1777

My Best Friend,

It is now a long time since I had an opportunity of writing to you, and I fear you have suffered unnecessary anxiety on my account. In the morning of the 19th instant, the Congress were alarmed in their beds by a letter from Mr. Hamilton, one of General Washington's family, that the enemy was in possession of the ford over the Schuylkill and the boats, so that they had it in their power to be in Philadelphia before morning. The papers of Congress belonging to the Secretary's office, the War office, the Treasury office, &c., were before sent to Bristol. The President, and all the other gentlemen were gone that road, so I followed with my friend Mr. Marchant, of Rhode Island, to Trenton, in the Jerseys. We stayed at Trenton until the 21st, when we set off to Easton, upon the forks of Delaware. From Easton we went to Bethlehem, from thence to Reading, from thence to Lancaster, and from thence to this town, which is about a dozen miles over the Susquehannah river. Here Congress is to sit. In order to convey the papers with safety, which are of more importance than all the members, we were induced to take this circuit, which is near a hundred and eighty miles, whereas this town, by the direct road, is not more than eighty-eight miles from Philadelphia. This tour has given me an opportunity of seeing many parts of this country which I never saw before. . . .

III

～∾⌒∾～

FRANCE AND HOLLAND

Adams was appointed commissioner to France in 1777. As a diplomat for a new nation, he had a difficult career. He accomplished little during his first stint (1777-79), and when he returned to Paris in late 1779, following a highly successful service in the Massachusetts constitutional convention, he often quarreled with Charles Vergennees, the foreign minister of Louis XVI. His relationship with Benjamin Franklin, who was a beloved figure in France, was also rocky. However, Adams was prophetic in emphasizing the importance of enlisting the aid of the French navy, which would later turn the tide of the war.

In August of 1780 Adams moved to Amsterdam, having heard through his intelligence sources that he might be able to procure a loan for the United States. Congress quickly gave him power to negotiate, but his initial optimism turned to despair as he realized that the Dutch, fearing a British reprisal, were unlikely to help. It was not until the autumn of 1782, after the surrender of the British at Yorktown, that he at last got his loan. In 1783 Adams returned to France as one of the principal negotiators for the Treaty of Paris.

Passy, 12 April 1778

My Dearest Friend,

I am so sensible of the difficulty of conveying letters safe to you, that I am afraid to write any thing more than to tell you, that after all the fatigues and dangers of my voyage and journey, I am here in health.

The reception I have met in this kingdom has been as friendly, as polite, and as respectful, as was possible. It is the universal opinion of the people here, of all ranks, that a friendship between France and America is the interest of both countries, and the late alliance, so happily formed, is universally popular; so much so, that I have been told by persons of good judgement, that the government here would have been under a sort of necessity of agreeing to it, even if it had not been agreeable to themselves. The delights of France are innumerable. The politeness, the elegance, the softness, the delicacy, are extreme. In short, stern and haughty republican as I am, I cannot help loving these people for their earnest desire and assiduity to please.

It would be futile to attempt descriptions of this country, especially of Paris and Versailles. The public buildings and gardens, the paintings, sculpture, architecture, music, &c., of these cities have already filled many volumes. The richness, the magnificence and splendor are beyond all description. This magnificence is not confined to public buildings, such as churches, hospitals, schools, &c., but extends to private houses, to furniture, equipage, dress, and especially to entertainments. But what is all this to me? I receive but little pleasure in beholding all these things, because I cannot but consider them as bagatelles, introduced by time and luxury in exchange for the great qualities, and hardy, manly virtues of the human heart. I cannot help suspecting that the more elegance, the less virtue, in all times and countries. Yet I fear that even my own dear country wants the power and opportunity more than the inclination to be elegant, soft and luxurious.

All the luxury I desire in this world is the company of my dearest friend, and my children, and such friends as they delight in, which I have sanguine hopes I shall, after a few years, enjoy in peace.

I am, with inexpressible affection,

Yours, yours,
John Adams

———

Passy, 25 April 1778

My Dearest Friend,

Monsieur Chaumont has just informed me of a vessel bound to Boston, but I am reduced to such a moment of time, that I can only inform you that I am well, and enclose a few lines from Johnny to let you know that he is so. I have ordered the things you desired to be sent you, but I will not yet say by what conveyance, for fear of accidents.

If human nature could be made happy by any thing that can please the eye, the ear, the taste, or any other sense, or passion, or fancy, this country would be the region for happiness. But if my country were at peace, I should be happier among the rocks and shades of Penn's hill; and would cheerfully exchange all the elegance, magnificence, and sublimity of Europe, for the simplicity of Braintree and Weymouth.

To tell you the truth, I admire the ladies here. Don't be jealous. They are handsome, and very well educated. Their accomplishments are exceedingly brilliant, and their knowledge of letters and arts exceeds that of the English ladies, I believe.

Tell Mrs. Warren that I shall write her a letter, as she desired, and let her know some of my reflections in this country. My venerable colleague [Benjamin Franklin] enjoys a privilege here, that is much to be envied. Being seventy years of age, the ladies not only allow him to

embrace them as often as he pleases, but they are perpetually embracing him. I told him, yesterday, I would write this
to America.

Passy, 13 February 1779

My Dearest Friend,

Yours of 15th December was sent me yesterday by the
Marquis, whose praises are celebrated in all the letters from
America. You must be content to receive a short letter,
because I have not time now to write a long one. I have lost
many of your letters, which are invaluable to me, and you
have lost a vast number of mine. Barnes, Niles, and many
other vessels are lost.

I have received intelligence much more agreeable than
that of a removal to Holland; I mean that of being reduced
to a private citizen, which gives me more pleasure than you
can imagine. I shall therefore soon present before you your
own good man. Happy, happy indeed shall I be, once more
to see our fireside. I have written before to Mrs. Warren, and
shall write again now. Dr. J. is transcribing your Scotch
song, which is a charming one. Oh, my leaping heart!

I must not write a word to you about politics, because
you are a woman.

What an offence have I committed! A woman!

I shall soon make it up. I think women better than men,
in general, and I know, that you can keep a secret as well as
any man whatever. But the world doesn't know this.
Therefore if I were to write my sentiments to you, and the
letter should be caught and hitched into a newspaper, the
world would say, I was not to be trusted with a secret.

I never had so much trouble in my life as here, and yet
I grow fat. The climate and soil agree with me. So do the
cookery and even the manners of the people, of those of
them at least that I converse with, churlish republican as
some of you on your side the water call me. The English

have got at me in their newspapers. They make fine work of me—fanatic, bigot, perfect cipher, not one word of the language, awkward figure, uncouth dress, no address, no character, cunning, hard-hearted attorney; but the falsest of it all is, that I am disgusted with the Parisians. Whereas I admire the Parisians prodigiously. They are the happiest people in the world, I believe, and have the best disposition to make others so. If I had your ladyship and our little folks here, and no politics to plague me, and a hundred thousand livres a year rent, I should be the happiest being on earth.

———

Passy, 20 February 1779

In the margin are the dates of all the letters I have received from you [ten between March 25, 1778, and January 4, 1779]. I have written you several times that number. They are almost all lost, I suppose by yours. But you should consider, it is a different thing to have five hundred correspondents and but one. It is a different thing to be under an absolute restraint and under none. It would be an easy thing for me to ruin you and your children by an indiscreet letter, and what is more, it would be easy to throw our country into convulsions. For God's sake never reproach me again with not writing or with writing scrips. Your wounds are too deep. You know not, you feel not the dangers that surround me, nor those that may be brought upon our country. Millions would not tempt me to write you as I used. I have no security that every letter I write you will not be broken open, and copied, and transmitted to Congress and to English newspapers. They would find no treason nor deceit in them, it is true, but they would find weakness and indiscretion, which they would make as ill a use of.

There are spies upon every word I utter, and every syllable I write. Spies planted by the English, spies planted by stockjobbers, spies planted by selfish merchants, and spies planted by envious and malicious politicians. I have been all along aware of this, more or less, but more so now than ever. My life has been often in danger, but I never considered my reputation and character so much in danger as now. I can pass for a fool, but I will not pass for a dishonest or a mercenary man. Be upon your guard, therefore. I must be upon mine, and I will.

Passy, 20 February 1779

A new commission has arrived by which the Dr. [Franklin] is sole minister. Mr. Lee[7] continues commissioner for Spain, but I am reduced to the condition of a private citizen. The congress have not taken the least notice of me. On the 11th of September they resolved to have one minister only in France. On the 14th they chose the Dr. In October they made out his commission, the Alliance sailed on the 14th January, and in all that interval they never so much as bid me come home, bid me stay, or told me I had done well or done ill. Considering the accusation against Mr. Lee,[8] how unexpected it was, and how groundless it is, I should not be at all surprised if I should see an accusation against me for something or other, I know not what, but I see that all things are possible.

Of all the scenes I ever passed through, this is the most extraordinary. The delirium among Americans here is the most extravagant. All the infernal arts of stockjobbers, all the voracious avarice of merchants have mingled themselves with American politics here, disturbed their operations, distracted our councils, and turned our heads.

---

[7] Arthur Lee. American diplomat to Spain in 1777, he was unable to obtain either a treaty or foreign aid. In 1778, he, along with Benjamin Franklin and Silas Deane, arranged a commercial and military alliance with France.

[8] Lee, Deane, and Franklin quarreled continuously while in Paris. Lee eventually got the best of Deane, accusing him of profiteering. Deane was recalled to appear before Congress, but was unable to convince the body of his innocence. Adams arrived in France just after Deane departed. His favor was courted by the two remaining diplomats, Franklin and Lee, but Adams grew to distrust both of them.

The Congress, I presume, expect that I should come home, and I shall come accordingly. As they have no business for me in Europe, I must contrive to get some for myself at home. Prepare yourself for removing to Boston, into the old house, for there you shall go, and there I will draw writs and deeds, and harangue juries, and be happy.

Passy, 27 February 1779

The weather continuing fine, I went to Saint Denis, the little village about eight miles from this place, where are the tombs of all the kings and queens. The statues of all lie in state in marble. The church is called the royal Church of Saint Denis, is magnificent, and there is an apartment in a chamber, where the crowns and many other curiosities are preserved. It is curious to see such a collection of gold, ivory and precious stones; as there is every species, I suppose, that is mentioned in the Revelation. The diamonds and rubies glitter. But I confess I have so much of the savage sachem in me, that these things make no great impression upon me. There are several little crucifixes here, which the ecclesiastic, who showed them, told us, were made of bits of the true cross. This may be, for any thing that I know.

In my return, I took a circuit round by Montmartre, and dined at home with the Dr. [Franklin], who has a fit of the gout, but is getting better.

The situation in which my masters have left me puzzles me very much. They have said nothing to me. But one set of gentlemen write that I am to go to Spain, another to Holland, a third to Vienna; but, upon the whole, I believe they don't intend to send me to either, but leave me to stay here in a ridiculous situation, or return home if I can get there. I shall return unless I should receive, before the time arrives for the vessel to sail, orders which I can execute with honor, and with a prospect of rendering some service to the public. But of these last two points, I will judge for myself.

[Undated letter]

My Dear Portia,[9]

Yesterday we went to see the garden of the King, *Jardin du Roi,* and his cabinet of natural history, *cabinet d'histoire naturelle.* The cabinet of natural history is a great collection of metals, minerals, shells, insects, birds, beasts, fishes and precious stones. They are arranged in good order and preserved in good condition, with the name of every thing, beautifully written on a piece of paper, annexed to it. There is also a collection of woods and marbles. The garden is large and airy, affording fine walks between rows of trees. Here is a collection, from all parts of the world, of all the plants, roots and vegetables that are used in medicine, and indeed of all the plants and trees in the world. A fine scene for the studious youths in physic and philosophy. It was a public day. There was a great deal of company, and I had opportunity only to take a cursory view. The whole is very curious. There is a handsome statue of M. Buffon, the great natural historian, whose works you have, whose labors have given fame to this cabinet and garden. When shall we have in America such collections?[10] The collection of American curiosities that I saw at Norwalk, in Connecticut, made by Mr. Arnold, which he afterwards, to my great mortification, sold to [New York] Governor [William] Tyron, convinces me that our country affords as ample materials for collections of this nature as any part of the world. . . .

---

9 One of Adams's intimate nicknames for Abigail. Portia is the spirited heroine of Shakespeare's *The Merchant of Venice.*

10 Adams had a lifelong fascination of the natural sciences. He would later initiate the founding of the American Academy of Arts and Sciences.

Amsterdam, 18 December 1780

My Dearest Portia,

I have this morning sent Mr. Thaxter with my two sons to Leyden, there to take up their residence for some time, and there to pursue their studies of Latin and Greek under the excellent masters, and there to attend lectures of the celebrated professors, in that university. It is much cheaper there than here. The air is infinitely purer, and the company and conversation are better. It is perhaps as learned a university as any in Europe.

I should not wish to have children educated in the common schools in this country, where a littleness of soul is notorious. The masters are mean spirited wretches, pinching, kicking and boxing the children upon every turn. There is besides a general littleness arising from the incessant contemplation of stivers and duits, which pervades the whole people. Frugality and industry are virtues every where, but avarice and stinginess are not frugality. The Dutch say that without a habit of thinking of every duit before you spend it, no man can be a good merchant, or conduct trade with success. This I believe is a just maxim in general, but I would never wish to see a son of mine govern himself by it. It is the sure and certain way for an industrious man to be rich. It is the only possible way for a merchant to become the first merchant or the richest man in the place. But this is an object that I hope none of my children will ever aim at. It is indeed true, every where, that those who attend to small expenses are always rich.

I would have my children attend to duits and farthings as devoutly as the merest Dutchman upon earth, if such attention was necessary to support their independence. . . .

Amsterdam, 2 December 1781

. . . Dear Tom[11] [Thomas, Adams's youngest child], thy letter does thee much honor. Thy brother Charles shall teach thee French and Dutch at home. I wish I could get time to correspond with thee and thy sister [Abigail, Adams's oldest child] more regularly, but I cannot. I must trust Providence and thine excellent mamma for the education of my children. Mr. Dana and our son are well at Petersburg. Hayden has some things for you. I hope he is arrived. I am sorry to learn you have a sum of paper. How could you be so imprudent? You must be frugal, I assure you. Your children will be poorly off. I can but barely live in the manner that is indispensably demanded of me by every body. Living is dear indeed here. My children will not be so well left by their father as he was by his. They will be infected with the examples and habits and tastes for expensive living without the means. He was not. My children shall never have the smallest soil of dishonor or disgrace brought upon them by their father, no, not to please ministers, kings or nations. At the expense of a little of this, my children might perhaps ride at their ease through life, but dearly as I love them, they shall live in the service of their country, in her navy, her army, or even out of either in the extremest degree of poverty, before I will depart in the smallest iota from my sentiments of honor and delicacy; for I, even I, have sentiments of delicacy as exquisite as the proudest minister that ever served a monarch. They may not be exactly like those of some ministers.

I beg you would excuse me to my dear friends, to whom I cannot write so often as I wish. I have indispensable duties which take up all my time, and require more than I have.

General Washington has done me great honor and much public service by sending me authentic accounts of his own

---

[11] This excerpt is found within a letter to Abigail.

and General [Nathaniel] Greene's last great actions. They are in the way to negotiate peace. It lies wholly with them. No other ministers but they and their colleagues in the army can accomplish the great event.

I am keeping house, but I want a housekeeper. What a fine affair it would be, if we could flit across the Atlantic as they say the angels do, from planet to planet! I would dart to Penn's hill and bring you over on my wings; but, alas, we must keep house separately for some time. But one thing I am determined on. If God should please to restore me once more to your fireside, I will never again leave it without your ladyship's company—not, not even to go to Congress at Philadelphia, and there I am determined to go, if I can make interest enough to get chosen, whenever I return. I would give a million sterling that you were here; and I could afford it as well as Great Britain can the thirty millions she must spend, the ensuing year, to complete her own ruin.

Farewell, farewell

IV

<p align="center">~~~~</p>

VICE PRESIDENT AND PRESIDENT

Adams served as Vice President throughout the Washington presidency (1789-97). He was generally frustrated by the job, as the VP had few responsibilities and little real power. He did, however, respect and admire the president, and he loyally supported his administration. When Washington announced he would not seek a third term in office, Adams, Alexander Hamilton, and Thomas Jefferson were considered the top contenders for the post. Although Adams often doubted the outcome, he handily won the election of 1796, thanks to the support of a solid New England.

His administration is generally viewed as a success. He handled many crises with skill and aplomb; dodging a war with France in 1798 was perhaps his biggest achievement. He also managed to avoid being dominated by his own Federalist Party in their contest against the rising popularity of the Jeffersonians. His last official act as president, and one that would resound for years, was the appointment of John Marshall to the Supreme Court. During his long reign as Chief Justice, Marshall raised the Court from a position of relative ignominy to one of power and majesty.

39

Adams also made several tactical errors while in office, the results of which paved the way for his defeat in 1800. The first was his failure to immediately name a new cabinet, after the best men among those recruited by Washington—including Alexander Hamilton, John Jay, and Henry Knox—resigned. He was fearful of being disloyal to the still-living Washington, and in truth it may very well have caused a crisis within the Federalist Party. But as a result Alexander Hamilton, seeking to control the President, was able to woo three members of Adams's cabinet, and thus undermine his authority. Not helping matters, Adams spent nearly half of his administration governing from his farm in Quincy, Massachusetts, rather than from the seat of government in Philadelphia. This second error kept him out of the political loop, and contributed to the effectiveness of Hamilton's intrigue.

In the election of 1800 a schism in the Federalist Party served to ensure Adams's defeat. He lost to his once and future friend, Thomas Jefferson, and at last retired to his beloved farm.

Philadelphia, 12 February 1793

My Dearest Friend,

I received yesterday your kind favor of the 1st of this month, and thank you for its agreeable contents. I have now to congratulate you on the arrival of your son and daughter and two grandsons, in fine health, at New York. They have done wisely to fly from the evil to come in Europe; although it is somewhat dubious whether our fellow citizens will have the wisdom to abstain from similar evils in this country. My friend Malesherbes[12] is about to crown the end of his life with greater glory than he gained in his youth or middle age, though this was splendid. Such a character as that great magistrate ought to wish to die on so great a theatre in defence of his prince, and struggling against the disgrace which enthusiasm is about to bring upon the nation.

The spirit of ambition and of conquest, which the French republic in its cradle has already discovered, has alarmed England and Holland. France has been execrated in Europe for their ambition for universal monarchy; but the passion was imputed to their kings, Henry 4th and Louis 14th. But the people are already giving unequivocal proofs of an equal lust after a universal republic. The passion is, and always has been, in the people, the nation, and their leaders will ever be infected with it, whether they call them kings, or presidents, or citizens. I can only sigh at the prospect of calamities opening on the human race and pray God to avert them.

We have today a deep snow, which I hope will last till I can reach Quincy in a sleigh and there enjoy a felicity, which will never be allowed me any where else.

Tenderly yours,
J.A.

---

[12] French Minister of State. In 1792, at his own request, he was appointed a defender of Louis XVI in the king's trial. He was soon after arrested and guillotined as a royalist, along with his daughter and grandchildren.

Philadelphia, 19 December 1793

. . . Citizen Genêt[13] made me a visit yesterday while I was in Senate, and left his card. I shall leave mine at his hotel tomorrow, as several of the senators have already hastened to return their visits. But we shall be in an awkward situation with this minister. I write you little concerning public affairs, because you will have every thing in print. How a government can go on, publishing all their negotiations with foreign nations I know not. To me it appears as dangerous and pernicious as it is novel; but, upon this occasion it could not, perhaps, have been avoided. You know where, I think, was the error in the first concoction. But such errors are unavoidable when the people in crowds out of doors undertake to receive ambassadors, and to dictate to their supreme executive.

I know not how it is, but in proportion as danger threatens I grow calm. I am very apprehensive that a desperate anti-federal party will provoke all Europe by their insolence. But my country has, in its wisdom, contrived for me the most insignificant office that ever the invention of man contrived or his imagination conceived; and as I can do neither good nor evil, I must be borne away by others and meet the common fate. . . .

Philadelphia, 2 January 1794

My Dearest Friend,

Our anti-federal scribblers are so fond of rotations that they seem disposed to remove their abuse from me to the

---

[13] French diplomat, sent as minister to the United States in 1793. He worked actively to rally support for France, which was simultaneously in the throes of revolution and engaged in a war with European monarchies, including Great Britain. Despite support from many Americans who were sympathetic to France, Genêt could neither persuade President Washington to allow French privateers to use U.S. ports as bases nor convince him to support a suggested invasion of Spanish Florida.

President. Bache's paper, which is nearly as bad as Freneau's,[14] begins to join in concert with it to maul the President for his drawing rooms, levees, declining to accept of invitations to dinners and tea parties, his birth day odes, visits, compliments, &c. I may be expected to be an advocate for a rotation of objects of abuse and for equality in this particular. I have held the office of Libellee General long enough. The burden of it ought to be participated and equalized according to modern republican principles. . . .

***

Philadelphia, 2 January 1794

My Dearest Friend,

The anxiety you express in your kind letter of 31st December, which I received this morning, for your country and the happiness of your children, is very amiable. The prospects of this country are gloomy, but the situation of all Europe is calamitous beyond all former examples. At what time, and in what manner, and by what means, the disasters which are come, and seem to be coming on mankind, may be averted, I know not. Our own people have been imprudent, as I think, and are now smarting under the effects of their indiscretion; but this, instead of a consolation, is an aggravation of our misfortune. Mr. Genêt has been abusive on the President and all his ministers, beyond all measure of decency or obligations of truth, and in other respects not yet publicly investigated, his conduct has been such as to make it difficult to know what to do with him. But I cannot explain myself fully. You must wait for time to bring forth events and *eclaircissements.*

Mrs. Washington always inquires affectionately after your health, and I never forget to present your respects.

***

[14] Republican journalists Benjamin Franklin Bache (grandson of Adams's old nemesis) and Phillip Freneau often criticized both Washington and Adams.

The news of this evening is, that the Queen of France is no more [Marie Antoinette was guillotined on October 16, 1793]. When will savages be satiated with blood? No prospect of peace in Europe, and therefore none of internal harmony in America. We cannot well be in a more disagreeable situation than we are with all Europe, with all Indians, and with all Barbary rovers. Nearly one half the continent is in constant opposition to the other, and the President's situation, which is highly responsible, is very distressing, He made me a very friendly visit yesterday, which I returned today, and had two hours' conversation with him alone in his cabinet. The conversation, which was extremely interesting, and equally affectionate, I cannot explain even by a hint. But his earnest desire to do right and his close application to discover it, his deliberate and comprehensive view of our affairs with all the world, appeared in a very amiable and respectable light. The anti-federalists and the frenchified zealots have nothing now to do that I conceive of, but to ruin his character, destroy his peace, and injure his health. He supports all their attacks with great firmness, and his health appears to be very good. The Jacobins would make a sortie upon him in all the force they could muster, if they dared.

I run on and say nothing, so I will conclude.

Your ever affectionate
J.A.

Philadelphia, 19 April 1794

My Dearest Friend,

Senate has been three days in debate upon the appointment of Mr. Jay[15] to go to London. It has this day been deter-

---

15 John Jay, negotiator of the Treaty of Paris and the first Chief Justice of the Supreme Court. He was sent to England to resolve ongoing controversies and to prevent another war.

mined in his favor eighteen versus eight.

You cannot imagine what horror some persons are in, lest peace should continue. The prospect of peace throws them into distress. Their countenances lengthen at the least opening of an appearance of it. Glancing gleams of joy beam from their faces whenever all possibility of it seems to be cut off. You can divine the secret source of these feelings as well as I. The opposition to Mr. Jay has been quickened by motives which always influence every thing in an elective government. Pretexts are never wanting to ingenious men, but the views of all the principal parties are always directed to the election of the first magistrate. If Jay should succeed, it will recommend him to the choice of the people for President, as soon as a vacancy shall happen. This will weaken the hopes of the southern States for Jefferson. This I believe to be the secret motive of the opposition to him, though other things were alleged as ostensible reasons; such as, his monarchical principles, his indifference about the navigation of the Mississippi, his attachment to England, his aversion to France, none of which are well founded, and his holding the office of Chief Justice, &c. . . .

Philadelphia, 20 January 1796

. . . I am, as you say, quite a favorite. I am to dine today again. I am heir apparent, you know, and a succession is soon to take place. But, whatever may be the wish or the judgment of the present occupant, the French and the demagogues intend, I presume, to set aside the descent. All these hints must be secrets. It is not a subject of conversation as yet. I have a pious and a philosophical resignation to the voice of the people in this case, which is the voice of God. I have no very ardent desire to be the butt of party malevolence. Having tasted of that cup, I find it bitter, nauseous, and unwholesome.

I hope Copeland will find his six loads to complete the meadow, and take the first opportunity to cart or sled the manure from the yard at home up to the top of Stonyfield hill. The first season that happens fit for ploughing, should be employed in cross ploughing the ground at home over the way. The news of my mother's arm growing better has given me great pleasure. Of the four barrels of flour I have shipped to you, present one of them to my mother from me, with my duty and affection. Tell my brother [Peter Boylston Adams] I hope he has seen his error, and become a better friend of peace and good government than he has been somewhat inclined to be since the promulgation of the treaty.

I am, with affections, as every, your

J.A.

———————

Philadelphia, 15 February 1796

My Dearest Friend,

This morning I have your favor of the 3d, which raised my spirits again after the mortification of passing the whole of last week without one.

Benjamin [Bache] has grown very dull. No abuse—no lies—no terrors, no panics, no rant, in comparison of what he used to have.

The subject [the retirement of George Washington] which you think will excite all their feelings is well known to every body in public life, but is talked of by nobody but in confidence. I could name you, however, as good federalists, and as good men as any, who think and say that he will retire, and that they would if they were he. And who would not? I declare upon my honor I would. After twenty years of such service with such success, and with no obligation to any one, I would retire, before my constitution failed, before my memory failed, before I should grow peevish and fretful, irresolute or improvident. I would no longer put at hazard a character so dearly earned, at present so uncontaminated, but liable by the weakness of age to be impaired in a moment. He has, in the most solemn manner, sworn before many witnesses at various times and on several occasions, and it is now, by all who are in the secret, considered as irrevocable as the laws of Medes and Persians. Your comments to [Henry] Knox were perfectly delicate and perfectly wise. You need not tremble to think of the subject. In my opinion there is no more danger in the change, than there would be in changing a member of the senate, and whoever lives to see it, will own me to be a prophet. If Jay or even Jefferson (and one or the other it certainly will be) if the succession should be passed over, should be the man, the government will go on as well as ever. Jefferson could not stir a step in any other system than that which is begun. Jay would not wish it. The votes will run for three persons. Two, I have mentioned; the third, being the heir apparent, will not probably be wholly overlooked. If Jefferson and Jay are President and Vice-President, as is not improbable, the other retires without noise, or cries, or tears to his farm. If either of these two is President and the other [Adams himself] Vice-President, he retires without murmur or complaint to his farm forever.[16] If this other should be President and Jefferson or Jay Vice-President, four years more, if life last, of residence in Philadelphia will be his and your portion, after which we shall probably be desirous of imitating the example of the present pair; or if, by reason of strength and fortitude, eight years should be accomplished, that is the utmost limit of time, that I will ever continue in public life at any rate.

Be of good courage therefore, and tremble not. I see nothing to appal me, and I feel no ill forebodings or faint

---

[16] Adams felt no one but Washington had a public service record as distinguished as his own and consequently that another term as Vice President, under Jefferson or Jay, would be beneath him. He is stating here that he would rather retire. (It is important to remember that at the time the candidate who received the second-most votes was named Vice President.)

misgivings. I have not the smallest dread of private life nor of public. If private life is to be my portion, my farm and my pen shall employ the rest of my days.

The money of the country, the paper money is the most unpleasant object I see. This must have a remedy, and I fear it will be reserved for me to stem the torrent, a worse one than the western rebellion, or the opposition to the treaty.

This is all in confidence and affection.

J.A.

Philadelphia, 1 March 1796

Yesterday the President sent his carriage for me to go with the family to the theatre. The Rage and the Spoiled Child were the two pieces. It rained and the house was not full. I thought I perceived a little mortification. Mr. George Washington and his fair lady were with us. . . .

As to the subject of yours of the 20th, I am quite at my ease. I never felt less anxiety when any considerable change lay before me. Aut transit aut finit. I transmigrate or come to an end. The question is between living at Philadelphia or at Quincy; between great cares and small cares. I have looked into myself and see no meanness nor dishonesty there. I see weakness enough, but no timidity. I have no concern on your account but for your health. A woman *can* be silent, when she will.

After all, persuasion may overcome the inclination of the chief to retire. But, if it should, it will shorten his days, I am convinced. His heart is set upon it, and the turpitude of the Jacobins touches him more nearly than he owns in words. All the studied efforts of the federalists to counterbalance abuse by compliment don't answer the end.

I suspect, but don't know, that Patrick Henry, Mr. Jefferson, Mr. Jay, and Mr. Hamilton, will all be voted for. I ask no questions; but questions are forced upon me. I have had some conversations purposely sought, in order, as I believe, indeed as I know, to convince me that the federalists had no thoughts of overleaping the succession. The only question that labors in my mind is, whether I shall retire with my file-leader? I hate to live in Philadelphia in summer, and I hate still more to relinquish my farm. I hate speeches, messages, addresses and answers, proclamations, and such affected, studied, constrained things. I hate levees and drawing rooms. I hate to speak to a thousand people to whom I have nothing to say. Yet all this I can do. But I am too old to continue more than one, or at most more than two heats, and that is scarcely time enough to form, conduct and complete any very useful system. . . .

Philadelphia, 9 April 1796

. . . I am so fatigued and disgusted with the insipidity of this dull life, that I am half of a mind to vow that if Washington don't resign, I will. The old hero looks very grave of late. However, there is a high probability that I am upon my last year of public life, for if there should not be a choice by the people, I will not suffer a vote to be given for me in the House of Representatives. I will never serve in that high and responsible situation without some foundation of people to stand on. If I should be chosen Vice President only by a plurality, I will refuse. In short, there are so many probable cases in which I am determined to retire that the probability of it is, upon the whole, very strong. Indeed, I feel myself to be a fool to serve here at all. . . .

Philadelphia, 30 December 1796

My Dearest Friend,

The prospect that opens upon me presents troubles enough of every kind. I have made some inquiry concerning horses and carriages and find that a common chariot of the plainest sort cannot be had under twelve hundred dollars, and if you go to a little more ornament and elegance, you must give fifteen hundred. The President has a pair of horses to sell, one, nine, the other, ten years old, for which he asks a thousand dollars, and there is no probability of procuring a decent span for less than six hundred dollars. House rent, another indispensable article, will be extravagantly high. The plenty of paper has unsettled every thing. Nothing has a price. Every one asks and every one cheats as much as he can, I think. I wish I knew what would be asked for a chariot in Boston.

The President says he must sell something to enable him to clear out. When a man is about retiring from public life, and sees nothing but a ploughshare between him and the grave, he naturally thinks most upon that. When Charles the fifth resigned his empire and crown, he went to building his coffin. When I contemplated a retirement, I meditated the purchase of Mrs. Vesey's farm, and thought of building a tomb on my own ground adjoining to the burying yard. The President is now engaged in his speculations upon a vault which he intends to build for himself, not to sleep but to lie down in. So you see, my little head is made like two great heads, and I have ambitiously placed myself between them. Mrs. Blodget, who, I dare say, is more desirous that you should be Presidente than that I should be President, says she is afraid President Washington will not live long. I should be afraid too, if I had not confidence in his farm and his horse. He must be a fool, I think, who dies of chagrin when he has a fine farm and a Narraganset mare that paces, trots and canters. But I don't know but all men are such fools. I think a man had better wear than rust.

The boyish language of the emissaries from Monroe's academy is not confined to Boston market. Captain B——
is holding the same cant. John Adams must be an intrepid to encounter the open assaults of France and the secret plots of England in concert with all his treacherous friends

and open enemies in his own country. Yet I assure you he never felt more serene in his life.

Yours most tenderly,
J.A.

Philadelphia, 5 January 1797

My Dearest Friend,

I dined yesterday with Dr. Rush,[17] who desired me to send the enclosed oration upon a weak democrat whom he is pleased to call a great philosopher, astronomer and republican. We must put up with the vagaries of our flighty friend. Mr. and Mrs. Liston, the Britons, dined there, the first time I had met the lady. They are Scotch, genteel people. Mr. and Mrs. Regal dined there too. Mr. Regal brought a letter, you remember, from Mr. Adams. A man of sixty, perhaps, married to a handsome girl of thirty. A man of learning, but I presume enthusiastical. He talks much of the philosophy of Mr. Kant or Kent, or some such name, a German of great fame. He speaks of him sometimes very extravagantly. I heard him say that he thought Kant would make a third from Socrates and Jesus Christ.

Mankind seems to me to have lost their senses. . . .

---

[17] Benjamin Rush, Philadelphia's most famous physician, and a close friend of Adams.

Philadelphia, 11 January 1797

My Dearest Friend,

On Tuesday, when I waited, as usual, on Mrs. Washington, after attending the levee, she congratulated me very complaisantly and affectionately on my election, and went farther and said more than I expected. She said it gave them great pleasure to find that the votes had turned in my favor, &c. I doubted whether their prudence would have ventured so far. I believe it sincere. Kidd, however, the steward, was very active and busy for Jefferson. This was from jealousy of Briesler,[18] no doubt. He expected that Jefferson would have taken him, I suppose, and his principle was as good as McKean's. Gerry is steady, while so many prove as slippery as eels. . . .

The most unpleasant part of the prospect before me is that of remaining here until June or July. I can't see my grass and barley grow, nor my wall rise. I have, however, almost forgotten my farm. It appears very differently to me. It seems as if I ought not to think about it. The river is frozen so that nothing can get out. Besides, flour is dearer here than at Boston by one third. It has rained today like a flood, but the weather must be very warm, and continue so many days before the river can open. There is no probability of it for some time. If it opens in season, I shall send some grass seeds. I will not suffer the bushes I have cut down to grown again; but I shall not attend much to my farm. My whole time and thoughts must be devoted to the public.

I think of you and dream of you and long to be with you. But I suppose this must not be yet. My duty and love to all.

J.A.

---

[18] John Briesler, a family servant.

Philadelphia, 26 January 1797

My Dearest Friend,

I have only time to enclose you something. Dr. Priestley[19] breakfasted with me. I asked him whether it was his opinion that the French would ultimately establish a republican government. He said it was, and his opinion was founded upon the prophecy. France appeared to him to be one of the horns that were to fall off. He acknowledged, however, the uncertainty, and related a paragraph from a French writer who travelled in England immediately before the restoration of Charles the second. "That the people were much engaged in disputing about a form of government, but that all agreed there would never be any kings in England again."

When statesmen found their judgments upon prophecies I can never confide in their opinions.

Philadelphia, 9 February, 1797

My Dearest Friend,

The die is cast,[20] and you must prepare yourself for honorable trials.

I must wait to know whether Congress will do any thing or not to furnish my house. If they do not, I will have no house before next fall, and then a very moderate one, with very moderate furniture.

The prisoners from Algiers arrived yesterday in this city,

---

[19] Joseph Priestley, English theologian and scientist. His support of the French revolution aroused local prejudice, and in 1791 his house and library were destroyed. In 1794 he immigrated to the United States.

[20] Adams won the vote count and was named president-elect.

in good health and looking very well. Captain Stevens is among them. One woman rushed into the crowd and picked out her husband whom she had not seen for fourteen years.

I am, and ever shall be, yours and no other's,

J. A.

Philadelphia, 5 March 1797

My Dearest Friend,

Your dearest friend never had a more trying day than yesterday. [The day of his inauguration as President.] A solemn scene it was indeed, and it was made more affecting to me by the presence of the General [Washington], whose countenance was as serene and unclouded as the day. He seemed to me to enjoy a triumph over me. Methought I heard him say, "Ay! I am fairly out and you fairly in! See which of us will be happiest." When the ceremony was over, he came and made me a visit, and cordially congratulated me, and wished my administration might be happy, successful, and honorable.

It is now settled that I am to go into his house. It is whispered that he intends to take French leave tomorrow. I shall write you as fast as we proceed. My chariot is finished, and I made my first appearance in it yesterday. It is simple but elegant enough. My horses are young, but clever.

In the chamber of the House of Representatives was a multitude as great as the space could contain, and I believe scarcely a dry eye but Washington's. The sight of the sun setting full orbed, and another rising, though less splendid, was a novelty. Chief Justice Ellsworth administered the oath, and with great energy. Judges Cushing, Wilson, and Iredell, were present. Many ladies. I had not slept well the night before, and did not sleep well the night after. I was unwell and did not know whether I should get through or not. I did, however. How the business was received I know not, only I have been told that Mason, the treaty publisher, said we should lose nothing by the change, for he never heard such a speech in public in his life.

All agree that, taken altogether, it was the sublimest thing ever exhibited in America. I am, my dearest friend, most affectionately and kindly yours.

John Adams

Washington, 16 February 1801

My Dearest Friend,

Saturday night, nine o'clock, and not before, I received yours of 13th, and the letter to Thomas with it, brought here no doubt by mistake. I regret very much that you have not a gentleman with you. The skittish young colt with you is always timorous, but no harm will befall you or her, I trust. The weather and roads here on Saturday, Sunday, and today, are the finest we have seen this year.

The election will be decided this day in favor of Mr. Jefferson, as it is given out by good authority.

The burden upon me in nominating judges and consuls and other officers, in delivering over the furniture, in the ordinary business at the close of a session, and in preparing for my journey of five hundred miles through the mire, is and will be very heavy. My time will be all taken up. I pray you to continue to write me. My anxiety for you is a very distressing addition to all my other labors.

Our bishop gave us a good discourse yesterday, and every body inquired after you. I was able to tell them you had arrived on Friday night at Baltimore. I sleep the better for having the shutter open, and all goes on well. I pray God to bless and preserve you.

I give a feast today to Indian kings and aristocrats.

Ever
J.A.